Geologic Map of the Tucson and Nogales Quadrangles, Arizona, Scale 1:250,000: A Digital Database: USGS Open-File Report 2001-275

U.S. Department of the Interior, United States Geological Survey (USGS), et al., J. A. Peterson

The BiblioGov Project is an effort to expand awareness of the public documents and records of the U.S. Government via print publications. In broadening the public understanding of government and its work, an enlightened democracy can grow and prosper. Ranging from historic Congressional Bills to the most recent Budget of the United States Government, the BiblioGov Project spans a wealth of government information. These works are now made available through an environmentally friendly, print-on-demand basis, using only what is necessary to meet the required demands of an interested public. We invite you to learn of the records of the U.S. Government, heightening the knowledge and debate that can lead from such publications.

Included are the following Collections:

Budget of The United States Government
Presidential Documents
United States Code
Education Reports from ERIC
GAO Reports
History of Bills
House Rules and Manual
Public and Private Laws
Code of Federal Regulations
Congressional Documents
Economic Indicators
Federal Register
Government Manuals
House Journal
Privacy act Issuances
Statutes at Large

Geologic map of the Tucson and Nogales quadrangles (Arizona, scale 1:250,000): A Digital Database

By J.A. Peterson, J.R. Berquist, S.J. Reynolds, and S.S. Page-Nedell
Digital database by G.P. Oland[1] and D.M. Hirschberg[1]
Edited by G.J. Orris[2]

Open-File Report 01-275
Digital database version 1.0

2001
(original paper map was Plate 1, Open-File 90-276, published in 1990)

Approved for publication August 8, 2001

This report is preliminary and has not been reviewed for conformity with U.S. Geological Survey editorial standards or with the North American Stratigraphic Code. Any use of trade, product, or firm names is for descriptive purposes only and does not imply endorsement by the U.S. Government. The digital database is not meant to be used or displayed at any scale larger than 1:125,000 (for example, 1:100,000 or 1:24,000).

U.S. DEPARTMENT OF THE INTERIOR
U.S. GEOLOGICAL SURVEY

[1] University of Arizona, 520 N. Park Ave., Tucson, Arizona 85719
[2] U.S. Geological Survey, 520 N. Park Ave., Tucson, Arizona 85719

Table of Contents

Figures

Tables

Introduction

The geologic map of the Tucson-Nogales 1:250,000 scale quadrangle (Peterson and others, 1990) was digitized by U.S. Geological Survey staff and University of Arizona contractors at the Southwest Field Office, Tucson, Arizona, in 2000 for input into a geographic information system (GIS). The database was created for use as a basemap in a decision support system designed by the National Industrial Minerals and Surface Processes project. The resulting digital geologic map database can be queried in many ways to produce a variety of geologic maps. Digital base map data files (topography, roads, towns, rivers and lakes, etc.) are not included; they may be obtained from a variety of commercial and government sources. Additionally, point features, such as strike and dip, were not captured from the original paper map and are not included in the database. This database is not meant to be used or displayed at any scale larger than 1:250,000 (for example, 1:100,000 or 1:24,000). The digital geologic map graphics and plot files that are provided in the digital package are representations of the digital database. They are not designed to be cartographic products.

The map area is located in Southern Arizona (fig. 1), just north of the border with Mexico. This report describes the methods used to convert the geologic map data into a digital format, the ArcInfo GIS file structures and relationships, and explains how to download the digital files from the U.S. Geological Survey public access World Wide Web site on the Internet.

List of Map Units

Qta Alluvium and sedimentary rock (Holocene to Middle Miocene) —Unconsolidated to well-consolidated and caliche-cemented sand, silt, and gravel and dissected basin-fill deposits of conglomerate, sandstone, and siltstone with minor lacustrine rocks. Includes Quiburis Formation, Ft. Lowell Formation, and parts of Rillito Andesite (Brown, 1939) and Nogales and Big Dome Formations

Tsm Sedimentary rocks (Middle and Early Miocene) —Conglomerate and sandstone that largely postdate the main pulse of middle Tertiary volcanism and that were deposited during middle Tertiary tectonism. Includes lower part of Rillito Andesite (Brown, 1939), Nogales Formation, San Manuel Formation, Ripsey Wash sequence, Hell Hole Conglomerate, Apsey Conglomerate, and lower part of Big Dome Formation

Tb Basaltic volcanic rocks (Middle Miocene to Oligocene) —Generally flat-lying to gently dipping flows of basalt and basaltic andesite, with interbedded sedimentary rocks and tuff

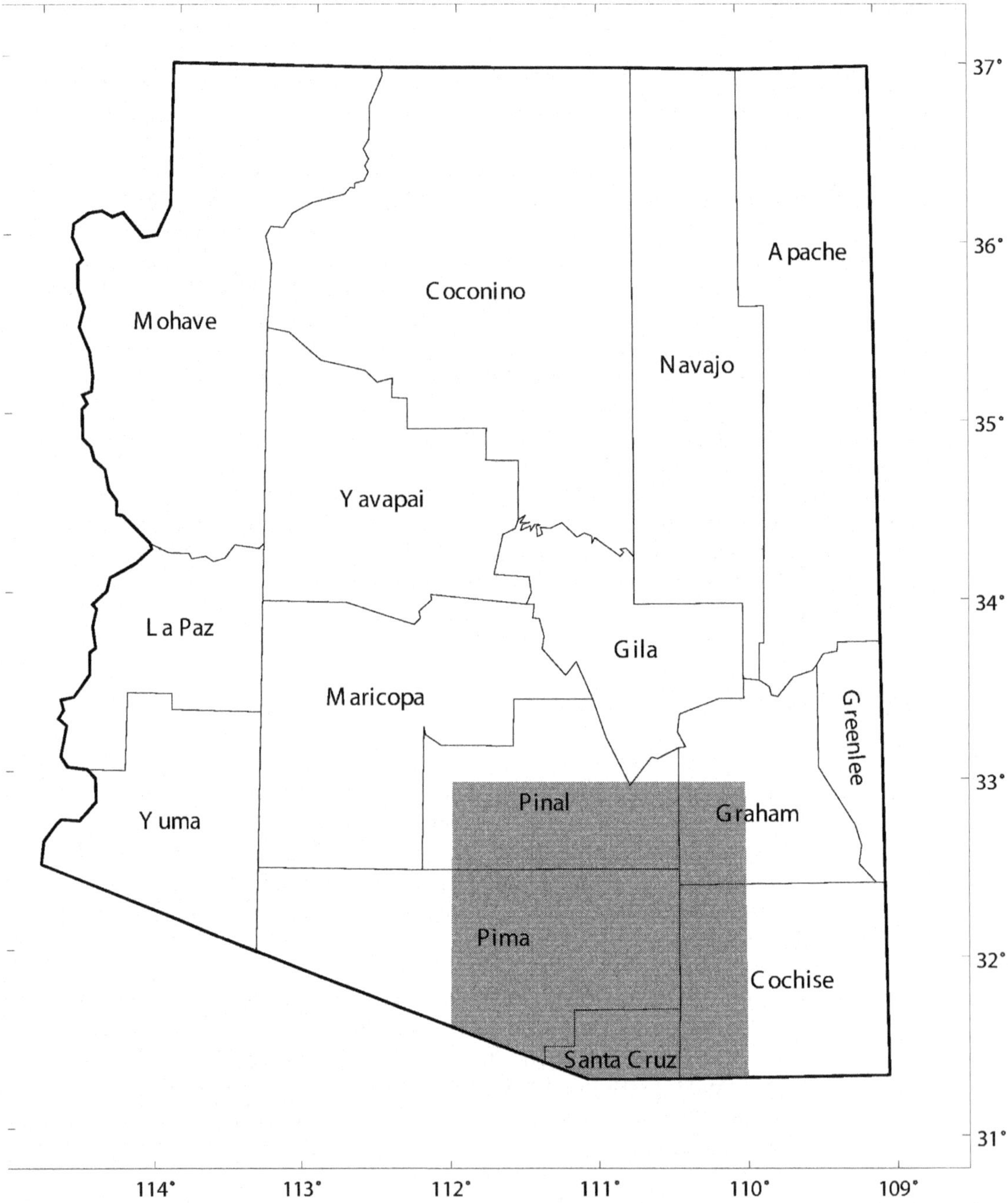

Figure 1. Index map showing the geographic extent of the mapped area (shaded fill) with respect to Arizona counties

Tsv Sedimentary, volcaniclastic, and volcanic rocks, undivided (Early Miocene and Oligocene) —Sedimentary and volcaniclastic rocks interbedded with middle Tertiary volcanic rocks. Includes Cloudburst Formation and equivalent rocks, and Wymola Conglomerate (Shafiqullah and others, 1976) near Picacho Peak

Tv Volcanic rocks, undivided (Early Miocene and Oligocene) —Includes (1) flows of basalt, andesite, and trachyandesite; (2) lava flows, flow breccia, and ash-flow tuff of rhyolitic, latitic, and dacitic composition; (3) potassium-metasomatized volcanic rocks at Picacho Peak; and (4) subordinate, interbedded sedimentary rocks

Tr Rhyolitic volcanic rocks (Early Miocene and Oligocene) —Rhyolitic, latitic, and dacitic lava flows and intrusive rocks with volcanic textures. Includes interbeds of pyroclastic and reworked pyroclastic rocks

Trt Rhyolitic tuff (Early Miocene and Oligocene) —Rhyolitic, latitic, and dacitic ash-flow tuff with local ash-flow and tuffaceous sedimentary rocks. Includes several members of Galiuro Volcanics and Recortado ash flow (Bikerman, 1967)

Ta Andesitic volcanic rocks (Early Miocene and Oligocene) —Andesite, trachyandesite, and dacite lava flows, agglomerate, and interbedded subordinate clastic and pyroclastic rocks. Includes coarsely plagioclase-porphyritic andesite, informally referred to as a "turkey-track" porphyry

Ti Subvolcanic intrusive rocks (Early Miocene and Oligocene) —Basaltic to rhyolitic or aplitic dikes, sills, and plugs with a volcanic or fine-grained granitic texture

Tg Granitoid rocks (Early Miocene and Oligocene)--Generally medium-grained biotite granodiorite and granite

Tm Mylonitic rocks (Early Miocene and Oligocene) —Mylonitic gneiss and schist exposed beneath Catalina and Picacho detachment faults. Formed by Tertiary mylonitization of Proterozoic crystalline rocks and Tertiary granitoid rocks

Tso Sedimentary rocks (Oligocene and latest Eocene) —Conglomerate, sandstone, siltstone, and lacustrine rocks deposited prior to main pulse of middle Tertiary volcanism. Includes Whitetail Conglomerate, Pantano Formation, Mineta Formation (Dickinson and Shafiqullah, 1989) and Three Links Conglomerate

TKgm Peraluminous, generally muscovite-bearing granite (Eocene to Late Cretaceous) — Medium- to coarse-grained peraluminous granite with minor amounts of biotite, muscovite, and garnet. Associated with aplite and pegmatite. Includes Wilderness granite (Keith and others, 1980), Wrong Mountain Granite, granite of Derrio Canyon, Pan Tak Granite, and phases of Tea Cup Granodiorite and

Texas Canyon Quartz Monzonite

TKg Granitoid rocks (Paleocene and Late Cretaceous) —Generally medium- to fine-grained biotite-hornblende granodiorite, granite, diorite, and local gabbro. Commonly porphyritic and associated with copper mineralization. Includes Ruby Star Granodiorite, Amole Granite (Brown, 1939), Texas Canyon Quartz Monzonite, Leatherwood Quartz Diorite (Bromfield, 1952), granodiorite of Chirreon Wash, quartz monzonite of Mineral Butte, granite of Sacaton Peak, Copper Creek Granodiorite, and phases of Tea Cup Granodiorite

TKs Sedimentary rocks (Paleocene and Late Cretaceous) —Conglomerate, sandstone, siltstone, and shale, locally of a volcaniclastic nature. Includes Claflin Ranch Formation (Richard and Courtright, 1960) and Cascabel formation

Tki Intrusive rocks, undivided (Early Tertiary and Late Cretaceous) —Dikes, sills, and other intrusions of rhyolite to andesite. Includes Amole Latite (Brown, 1939) and porphyritic biotite rhyodacite in Comobabi Mountains

TKv Volcanic rocks, undivided (Paleocene and Late Cretaceous) —Andesitic, dacitic, and rhyolitic lava flows, pyroclastic rocks, and local subvolcanic intrusions. Includes Glory Hole Volcanics, Williamson Canyon Volcanics, Muleshoe volcanics, Roskruge Volcanics, and numerous units in the Tucson Mountains, such as the Tucson Mountain Chaos (Courtright, 1958) and andesite megabreccia blocks hosted in a matrix of rhyolitic ash-flow tuff (Cat Mountain Rhyolite (Brown, 1939)

TKr Rhyolitic volcanic rocks (Paleocene and Late Cretaceous) —Rhyolitic to dacitic flows, tuff, volcaniclastic rocks, and subvolcanic intrusions. Includes tuff of Confidence Peak, Mount Lord Volcanics, and Cat Mountain Rhyolite (Brown, 1939)

Ks Sedimentary rocks (Cretaceous) —Conglomerate, sandstone, and finer grained rocks including American Flag Formation, Pinkard Formation, and rocks of uncertain affinity in southern Winchester Mountains

Kv Volcanic rocks (Cretaceous) —Andesite flows and tuffs with intercalated diorite rocks and conglomerate. Rhyodacitic tuffs and flows locally intensely silicified

Kg Granitoid rocks (Cretaceous) —Porphyritic granodiorite stocks

KJb Bisbee Group and related rocks (Early Late Cretaceous to Late Jurassic)--Sandstone, siltstone, shale, conglomerate, and limestone. Includes Glance Conglomerate and other units of Bisbee Group, Amole Arkose (Brown, 1939), Sand Wells Formation, and correlative rocks in Roskruge, Silver Bell, and Santa Rosa Mountains

KJs Sedimentary rocks, undifferentiated (Cretaceous and Jurassic) — Sandstone, siltstone, and conglomerate in Waterman Mountains. Probably contains rocks equivalent to units KJb and Js

Js Sedimentary rocks (Jurassic) —Sandstone, siltstone, conglomerate, and their metamorphic equivalents, including phyllite, quartzite, and schist

Jvs Volcanic and sedimentary rocks, undivided (Jurassic) —Rhyolitic flows and tuff, andesitic to trachyandesitic flows and flow breccia, interbedded with mudstone, siltstone, sandstone, and conglomerate. Includes Walnut Gap Volcanics and Sil Nakya and Cocoraque Formations

Jv Volcanic rocks (Jurassic) —Rhyolitic, dacitic, and andesitic volcanic flows, flow breccia, and tuff, with local sedimentary rocks

Ja Andesitic volcanic rocks (Jurassic) —Andesitic to trachyandesitic flows, flow breccia, tuff, and associated sedimentary rocks

Jg Granitoid rocks (Jurassic) —Coarse- to fine-grained granite, granodiorite, quartz syenite, syenodiorite, diorite, and rhyolite, rhyolite porphyry, and aplite intrusions

Jm Metamorphic rocks (Jurassic) —Schistose rocks of volcanic, sedimentary, and uncertain origin

Pzs Sedimentary rocks, undifferentiated (Paleozoic) — Limestone, dolomite, sandstone, quartzite, siltstone, shale, and conglomerate commonly metamorphosed to low grade

PPs Sedimentary rocks (Permian and Pennsylvanian) —Limestone, dolomite, sandstone, siltstone, and conglomerate of Naco Group

Ps Sedimentary rocks (Permian) —Limestone, dolomite, sandstone, and quartzite of upper part of Naco Group. Includes Rainvalley Formation, Concha Limestone, Scherrer Formation, Epitaph Dolomite, and Colina Limestone

Ps Sedimentary rocks (Pennsylvanian) —Limestone, dolomite, sandstone, siltstone, and conglomerate of lower part of Naco Group. Includes Earp and Horquilla Formations

MDs Sedimentary rocks (Mississippian and Devonian) —Limestone and dolomite with minor shale, siltstone, sandstone, and conglomerate. Includes Black Prince Formation, Escabrosa Limestone, and Martin Formation

€s Sedimentary rocks (Cambrian) —Quartzite, sandstone, shale, conglomerate, limestone, and dolomite. Includes Abrigo Formation and Bolsa Quartzite

YP̶zs Sedimentary rocks, undivided (Paleozoic and Middle Proterozoic) — Includes Paleozoic sedimentary rocks and Proterozoic Apache Group, with local diabase

Ydb Diabase (Middle Proterozoic) —Dikes and sills of fine- to coarse-grained diabase and associated rocks

Ya Apache Group (Middle Proterozoic) —Quartzite, siltstone, mudstone, limestone, and conglomerate. Includes Troy Quartzite, Mescal Limestone, Dripping Spring Formation, and Pioneer Formation

Yg Granite (Middle Proterozoic) —Coarse- to medium-grained granite and granodiorite, commonly with megacrysts of K-feldspar. Includes 1.45 Ga Oracle Granite (Peterson, 1938), Ruin Granite and Tungsten King Granite. Many outcrops contain dikes of pegmatite, alaskite, and aplite

Xg Granite (Early Proterozoic) —Undeformed to foliated, medium-grained granodiorite, granite, and quartz diorite. Includes 1.65 Ga Johnny Lyon Granodiorite and correlative rocks

Xm Metamorphic rocks, undivided (Early Proterozoic) —Greenschist to lower-amphibolite-facies metasedimentary, metavolcanic, metahypabyssal, and metaplutonic rocks

Xms Metasedimentary rocks (Early Proterozoic) —Schist, phyllite, metasandstone, and quartzite, with some metaconglomerate and metavolcanic rocks

Xmv Metavolcanic rocks (Early Proterozoic) —Schist, greenstone, and foliated and metamorphosed rhyolitic, dacitic, and andesitic flows, flow breccia, and tuff

Data Sources, Processing, and Accuracy

U.S. Geological Survey staff and contractors of the Southwest Field Office digitized the lines and polygons of the Tucson-Nogales map from a scanned image of a mylar created for Open-File Report 90-276; point features, such as strike and dip, were not captured. The digitized map was then edited to faithfully represent the geology (exclusive of point features) shown on the published paper geologic map (Peterson and others, 1990). Problems resulting from unlabeled units, missing contacts, extra contacts, and other geologic inconsistencies were resolved by G.J. Orris using other published and unpublished geologic maps of the area and geologic reasoning to keep the changes as consistent as possible with the rest of the original map. These sources include Beikman and others (1995), Berquist and others (1978), Haxel and others (1978), and Keith and Theodore (1975). Peterson and others (1990) compiled the source map geology from Bikerman (1967), Bromfield (1952), Brown (1939), Courtright (1958), Dickenson and Shafiqullah (1989), Keith and others (1980), Peterson (1938), Richard and Courtright (1960), and Shafiqullah and others (1976), among many other sources.

The overall accuracy, with respect to the location of the lines, of the digital geologic map is probably no better than approximately ± 200 m. This digital database is not meant to be used or displayed at any scale larger than 1:250,000 (for example, 1:100,000 or 1:24,000).

More information is now known about the geology of southern Arizona than was known at the time the map was originally compiled. Among the geologic problems associated with the original compilation are the following problems

(B. Houser, written commun., December, 1, 2000):

- Basalt is listed as one of the lithologics present in the unit Tv, Tertiary volcanic rocks. There are no early Miocene or Oligocene rocks of basaltic composition in southeastern Arizona.
- The list of formations that compose Cretaceous sedimentary rocks, Ks, should include the Salero and Fort Crittenden Formations, which are found on the east and west sides of the Santa Rita Mountains.

GIS Documentation

The Tucson-Nogales Digital Geologic Database consists of one ArcInfo dataset: TN250K (geologic structure). The relationships between this dataset and its respective look-up (related) tables are illustrated in Figure 2. The TN250K dataset contains the arcs representing contacts, faults, and linear geologic units (dikes), and the polygons representing the areal geologic rock units. Appendix A has the list of the digital files in the Open-File Report. Appendix B contains the metadata for the digital geologic map database.

Linear Features

Descriptions of the items identifying linear features such as contacts, boundaries (for example, lines of latitude and longitude, state boundaries) and structures are in the arc attribute table, TN250K.AAT (table 1). Attribute descriptions for items in the contact and boundary look-up table, TN250K.CON may be found in table 2. Table 3 contains attribute descriptions for items in the structure look-up table, TN250K.STR (for use with the GEOL_DIA.LIN lineset), and table 4 lists the attribute descriptions for items in the linear geologic unit look-up table, TN250K.LGU (also for use with the GEOL_DIA.LIN lineset).

Areal Features

Table 5 contains descriptions of the items identifying geologic units in the polygon attribute table, TN250K.PAT, and attribute descriptions for items in the lithology (rock unit) look-up table, TN250K.RU, are listed in table 6.

Source Attributes

Descriptive source or reference information for the TN250K ArcInfo dataset is stored in TN250K.REF; attribute descriptions for items in these files are listed in table 7.

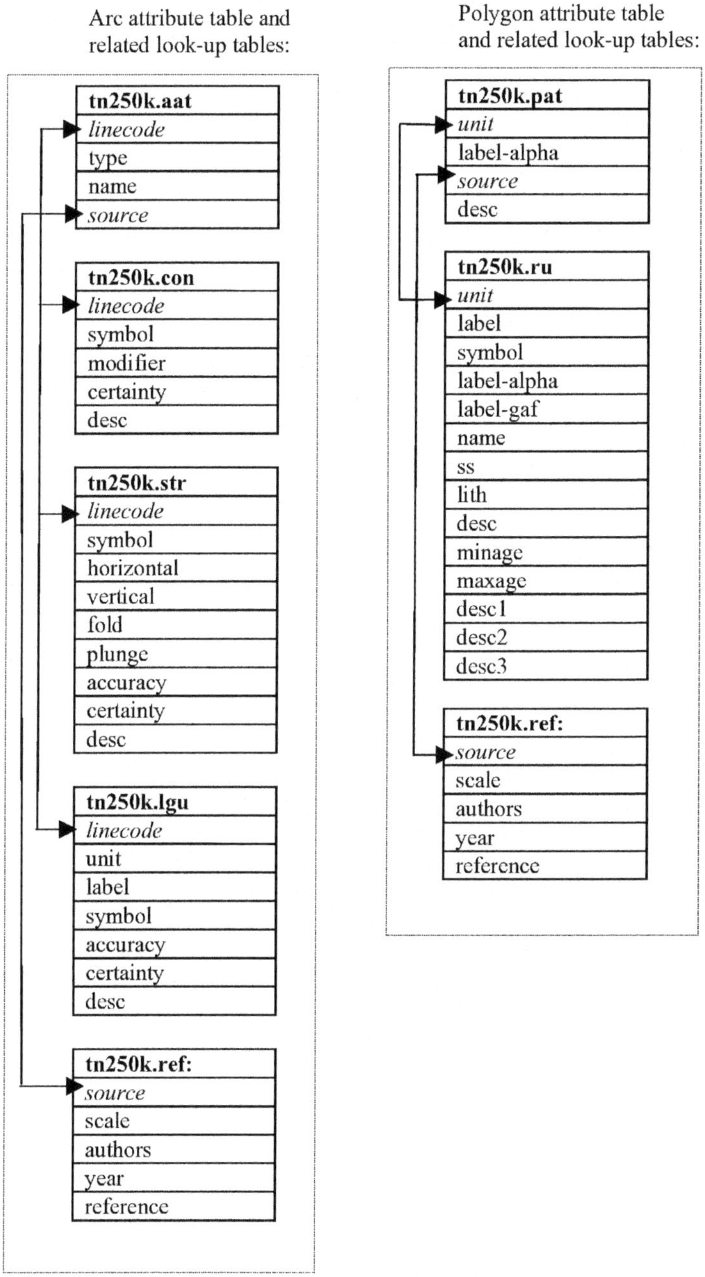

Figure 2. Relationships between feature attribute tables and look-up tables.

Table 1. Arc attribute table-- TN250K.AAT

ITEM NAME	ITEM TYPE	ITEM WIDTH	ATTRIBUTE DESCRIPTION
linecode	integer	3	Numeric code used to identify type of linear feature. Linecodes < 100 are used for contacts and boundaries, which are described in the tn250k.con file. Linecodes > 100 and < 600 represent structural features, which are described in the tn250k.str file. Linecodes > 600 refer to linear geologic units (dikes and sills), which are described in the tn250k.lgu file.
type	character	15	Basic feature type.
name	character	30	Name, if any, given to structural feature.
source	integer	4	Numeric code used to identify the data source for the linear feature. Complete references for the sources are listed in the tn250k.ref file.

Table 2. Contact look-up table-- TN250K.CON

ITEM NAME	ITEM TYPE	ITEM WIDTH	ATTRIBUTE DESCRIPTION
linecode	integer	3	Numeric code (a value < 100) used to identify type of contact or boundary. (This item also occurs in tn250k.aat).
symbol	integer	3	Line symbol number used by ArcInfo to plot lines. Symbol numbers refer to the geol_dia.lin lineset
modifier	character	20	Line type modifier, that is, approximate, concealed, gradational. No entry implies 'known.'
certainty	character	15	Degree of certainty of contact or boundary, that is, inferred, uncertain. No entry implies 'certain.'
desc	character	100	Written description or explanation of contact or boundary.

Table 3. Structure look-up table-- TN250K.STR			
ITEM NAME	ITEM TYPE	ITEM WIDTH	ATTRIBUTE DESCRIPTION
linecode	integer	3	Numeric code (a value > 100 and < 600) used to identify type of structural feature. (This item also occurs in tn250k.aat).
symbol	integer	3	Line symbol number used by ArcInfo to plot arcs. Symbol numbers refer to the geol_dia.lin lineset.
horizontal	character	20	Type of horizontal fault movement, for example, left-lateral, right-lateral.
vertical	character	20	Type of vertical fault movement, for example, normal.
fold	character	15	Type of fold, for example, anticline, syncline.
plunge	character	15	Type of plunge on fold, that is, horizontal, plunging, plunging in, plunging out.
accuracy	character	15	Line type modifier indicating degree of accuracy, that is, approximately located, concealed, gradational. No entry implies 'known.'
certainty	character	15	Degree of certainty of contact or boundary, that is, inferred, uncertain. No entry implies 'certain.'
desc	character	100	Written description or explanation of structural feature.

Table 4. Linear geologic unit look-up table-- TN250K.LGU			
ITEM NAME	ITEM TYPE	ITEM WIDTH	ATTRIBUTE DESCRIPTION
linecode	integer	3	Numeric code (a value > 600) used to identify type of linear geologic unit (rock unit). (This item also occurs in TN250K.AAT).
unit	integer	4	Numeric code used to identify the geologic unit, which is described in the tn250k.ru look-up table (this item also occurs in the tn250k.ru table).
label	character	10	Map label used in the map proper to identify geologic unit.
symbol	integer	3	Line symbol number used by ArcInfo to plot arcs. Symbol numbers refer to the geol_dia.lin lineset.
accuracy	character	15	Line type modifier indicating degree of accuracy, that is, approximately located, concealed, gradational. No entry implies 'known.'
certainty	character	15	Degree of certainty of contact or boundary, that is, inferred, uncertain. No entry implies 'certain.'
desc	character	100	Written description of linear geologic unit.

Table 5. Geologic unit look-up table-- TN250K.PAT			
ITEM NAME	ITEM TYPE	ITEM WIDTH	ATTRIBUTE DESCRIPTION
unit	integer	4	Numeric code used to identify the rock unit, which is described in the tn250k.ru look-up table.
label-alpha	character	10	Rock unit label (abbreviation) used to label unit on map with standard alphabetic characters.
source	integer	4	Numeric code used to identify the data source for the rock unit. Complete references for the sources are listed in the tn250k.ref file.
desc	character	250	Formal or informal unit name.

Table 6. Lithology look-up table-- TN250K.RU			
ITEM NAME	ITEM TYPE	ITEM WIDTH	ATTRIBUTE DESCRIPTION
unit	integer	4	Numeric code used to identify rock unit (this item also occurs in tn250k.pat).
label	character	10	Rock unit label (abbreviation) used to label unit on the map. This item was calculated equal to 'label-gaf'.
symbol	integer	3	Shadeset symbol number used by ArcInfo to plot a filled/shaded polygon. The symbol numbers used in this file refer to the wpgcmyk.shd shadeset.
label-alpha	character	10	Rock unit label (abbreviation) for use with standard alphabetic characters (for example, TR for Triassic).
label-gaf	character	10	Rock unit label (abbreviation) that uses the geoageFullAlpha font, version 1.1.
name	character	7	The prefix portion of the rock unit label that does not include subscripts. (If subscripting is not used in the original unit label, then the 'name' entry is the same as the 'label-alpha' entry.)
ss	character	3	The suffix portion of the geologic unit label that includes subscripts. No entry implies no subscript.
lith	character	20	Major type of lithostratigraphic unit
desc	character	250	Formal or informal unit name
minage	character	7	Minimum stratigraphic age of lithologic unit, for example, CRET - Cretaceous, TERT - Tertiary, PREC - Precambrian.
maxage	character	7	Maximum stratigraphic age of lithologic unit.
desc1	character	200	Explanation of rock unit.
desc2	character	200	Continuation of desc1 field if needed.
desc3	character	200	Continuation of desc2 field if needed.

Table 7. Source information look-up table-- TN250K.REF			
ITEM NAME	ITEM TYPE	ITEM WIDTH	ATTRIBUTE DESCRIPTION
source	integer	4	Numeric code used to identify the data source. (This item also occurs in the tn250k.aat and tn250k.pat files.)
scale	integer	10	Scale of source map. (This value is the denominator of the proportional fraction that identifies the scale of the map that was digitized or scanned to produce the digital map.)
authors	character	200	Author(s) or compiler(s) of source map entered as last name, first name or initial, and middle initial.
year	integer	4	Source (map) publication date
reference	character	250	Remainder of reference in USGS reference format.

Obtaining the Digital Database

The complete database for the digital geologic map of the Tucson and Nogales Quadrangles is available in ArcInfo interchange format with associated data files. These data and map images are maintained in a Universal Transverse Mercator projection with the following parameters:

zone:	12
spheroid:	Clarke, 1866
false easting (meters):	0.00
false northing (meters):	0.00

To obtain copies of the digital data, do one of the following:

1) Users may download the digital files from the USGS public access World Wide Web site on the Internet:
URL = http://geopubs.wr.usgs.gov/open-file/of01-275/ or

2) Users can use Anonymous FTP to obtain the digital files from the directory pub/open-file/of01-275 at geopubs.wr.usgs.gov.

The Internet sites contain the complete database for the digital geologic map of the Tucson and Nogales Quadrangles. To manipulate these data in a geographic information system (GIS), you must have a GIS that is capable of reading ArcInfo interchange-format files.

Obtaining Paper Maps

Paper copies of the digital geologic map are not available from the USGS. However, with access to the Internet and access to a large-format (36") color plotter that can interpret either PDF (portable document format) , or EPS (encapsulated postscript) files, a 1:250,000-scale paper copy of the geologic map can be made as follows:
1. Download the digital version of the map, tn250k.pdf or tn250k.eps, from the USGS public access World Wide Web site on the Internet using the
URL = http://geopubs.wr.usgs.gov/open-file/of01-275
or
2. Anonymous FTP the plot file, tn250k.pdf or tn250k.eps, from: geopubs.wr.usgs.gov, in the directory:
pub/open-file/of01-275
3. This file can be plotted by any large-format color plotter that can interpret EPS or PDF files. The map dimensions are 38.5" by 35.0", landscape orientation.

References Cited

Beikman, H.M, Haxel, G.B., and Miller, R.J., 1995, Geologic map of the Tohono O'Odham Indian Nation, southern Arizona: U.S Geological Survey Miscellaneous Investigations Map I-2017, 2 sheets, scale 1:125,000.

Bergquist, J.R., Blacet, P.M., and Miller, S.T., 1978, Reconnaissance geologic map of the Santa Rosa Mountains Quadrangle, Pima County, Arizona: U.S. Geological Survey Miscellaneous Field Studies Map MF- 935, scale 1:62,500.

Bikerman, Michael, 1967, Isotopic studies in the Roskruge Mountains, Pima County, Arizona: Geological Society of America Bulletin, v. 78, p. 1029-1036.

Bromfield, C.S., 1952, Some geologic features of the Santa Catalina Mountains: Tucson, Arizona, Arizona Geological Society Guidebook, p. 50-55.

Brown, W.H., 1939, Tucson Mountains and Arizona basin range type: Geological Society of America bulletin, v. 50, p. 697-760.

Courtright, J.H., 1958, Progress report on investigations of some Cretaceous-Tertiary formations in southeastern Arizona: Tucson, Arizona, Arizona Geological Society Digest, v. 1, p. 7-9.

Courtright, J.H., 1958, Progress report on investigations of some Cretaceous-Tertiary formations in southeastern Arizona: Tucson, Arizona, Arizona Geological Society Digest, v. 1, p. 7-9.

Dickinson, W.R., and Shafiqullah, Muhammad, 1989, K-Ar and F-T ages for syntectonic mid-Tertiary volcanosedimentary sequences associated with the Catalina core complex and San Pedro trough in southern Arizona: Isochron/West, no. 52, p. 15-27.

Drewes, H., 1980, Tectonic map of Southeast Arizona: U.S. Geological Survey Miscellaneous Investigations Series Map I- 1109, 2 sheets, scale 1:125,000.

Haxel, G., Briskey, J.A., Rytuba, J.J., Bergquist, J.R., Blacet, P.M., and Miller, S.T., 1978, Reconnaissance geologic map of the Comobabi Quadrangle, Pima County, Arizona: U.S. Geological Survey Miscellaneous Field Studies Map MF- 964, scale 1:62,500.

Keith, S.B., Reynolds, S.J., Damon, P.E., Shafiqullah, M., Livingston, D.E., and Pushkar, P.D., 1980, Evidence for multiple intrusion and deformation within the Santa Catalina-Rincon-Tortolita crystalline complex, southeastern Arizona, *in* Crittenden, M.D., Jr., Coney, P.J., and Davis, G.H., eds., Cordilleran metamorphic core complexes: Geological Society of America Memoir 153, p. 217-267.

Keith, W.J., and Theodore, T.G., 1975, Reconnaissance geologic map of the Arivaca Quadrangle, Arizona: U.S. Geological Survey Miscellaneous Field Studies Map MF-0678, scale 1:62,500.

Peterson, J.A., Berquist, J.R., Reynolds, S.J., and Page-Nedell, S.S., 1990, Plate 1-Geologic map of the Tucson and Nogales quadrangles, *in* Peterson, J.A., ed., Preliminary mineral resource assessment of the Tucson and Nogales 1° x 2° quadrangles, Arizona: U.S. Geological Survey Open-File Report 90-276, 134 p., 24 plates.

Peterson, N.P., 1938, Geology and ore deposits of the Mammoth mining camp area, Pinal County, Arizona: Arizona Bureau of Mines Bulletin 144, p. 8-9.

Richard, Kenyon, and Courtright, J.H., 1960, Some Cretaceous-Tertiary relationships in southeastern Arizona and New Mexico: Tucson, Arizona, Arizona Geological Society Digest, v. 3, p. 1-7.

Shafiqullah, M., Lynch, D.J., Damon, P.E., Pierce, H.W., 1976, Geology, geochronology, and geochemistry of the Picacho Peak area, Pinal County, Arizona: Tucson, Arizona, Arizona Geological Society Digest, v. 12, p. 202-260.

Appendix A - List of digital files in the Tucson and Nogales GIS

Report text in portable document format:
- tn250k.pdf

Primary ArcInfo interchange-format (*.e00) and metadata (*.met) files for the digital geology:
- tn250k.e00 - line and poly GIS
- tn250k.met - metadata

Adobe portable document format (*.pdf) and encapsulated postscript (*.eps) plot files for the geologic map sheet:
- tn-map.pdf
- tn-map.eps

Appendix B – Metadata file (tn250k.met) for the Tucson and Nogales GIS

Identification_Information:

Citation:
Citation_Information:
Originator: Peterson, J.A.
Originator: Berquist, J.R.
Originator: Reynolds, S.J.
Originator: Page-Nedell, S.S.
Originator: Orris, Greta J. (digital editor)
Originator: Oland, Paul (digital compiler)
Originator: Hirschberg, Douglas M. (digital compiler)
Publication_Date: 2001
Title: Geologic map of the Tucson and Nogales quadrangles (Arizona, scale 1:250,000):
A Digital Database Edition: version 1
Geospatial_Data_Presentation_Form: map
Series_Information:
Series_Name: U.S. Geological Survey Open-File Report
Issue_Identification: OFR 01-275
Publication_Information:
Publication_Place: Tucson, AZ
Publisher: U.S. Geological Survey
Online_Linkage: <http://geopubs.wr.usgs.gov/open-file/of01-275>

Description:

Abstract:

The Tucson-Nogales dataset was digitized by U.S. Geological Survey staff and contractors in the Southwest Field Office, Tucson, Arizona for input into an ArcInfo geographic information system (GIS); point features, such as strike and dip, were not captured.

Purpose:

This dataset was constructed to provide the Carbonate Resource Evaluation System (CRES) of the National Industrial Minerals and Surficial Processes Project with a southwest dataset to use to test the CRES tools.

Supplemental_Information:

Because the original map was a single color map, many of the polygons did not close or were not labeled. Dr. Orris used a variety of published and unpublished work to resolve these and other geologic problems with the original mapping.

Time_Period_of_Content:
 Time_Period_Information:
  Single_Date/Time:
   Calendar_Date: 1990
 Currentness_Reference: date of original map publication

Status:
 Progress: complete
 Maintenance_and_Update_Frequency: None planned

Spatial_Domain:
 Bounding_Coordinates:
  West_Bounding_Coordinate: -112.
  East_Bounding_Coordinate: -110.
  North_Bounding_Coordinate: 33.
  South_Bounding_Coordinate: 31.3

Keywords:
 Theme:
  Theme_Keyword_Thesaurus: None
  Theme_Keyword: geology
  Theme_Keyword: geologic map
 Place:
  Place_Keyword_Thesaurus: None
  Place_Keyword: Tucson
  Place_Keyword: Arizona
  Place_Keyword: Nogales

Access_Constraints: None

Use_Constraints:
 These data are not to be used at scales greater than 1:250,000.

 Any hardcopies utilizing these data sets shall clearly indicate their source. If the user has modified the data in any way they are obligated to describe the types of modifications they have performed on the hardcopy map. User specifically agrees not to misrepresent these data sets, nor to imply that changes they made were approved by the U.S. Geological Survey.

Point_of_Contact:
 Contact_Information:
  Contact_Person_Primary:
   Contact_Person: Dr. Greta J. Orris
   Contact_Organization: U.S. Geological Survey
  Contact_Position: Geologist
  Contact_Address:
   Address_Type: mailing and physical address
   Address: 520 N. Park Ave., Suite 355
   City: Tucson
   State_or_Province: AZ
   Postal_Code: 85719-5035
   Country: USA
  Contact_Voice_Telephone: 520-670-5583

Contact_Facsimile_Telephone: 520-670-5113
Contact_Electronic_Mail_Address: greta@usgs.gov

Data_Set_Credit:
G. Stephen Pitts provided invaluable assistance and advice on how to make this map digital and publish the result.

Native_Data_Set_Environment:
SunOS, 5.6, sun4u UNIX
ARCINFO version 7.2.1

Data_Quality_Information:
Attribute_Accuracy:
Attribute_Accuracy_Report:
Attribute accuracy was verified by manual comparison of hard copy plots of the digital dataset with the source materials.

Logical_Consistency_Report:
Polygon and chain-node topology present.
Polygons intersecting the neatline are closed along the border. Segments making up the outer and inner boundaries of a polygon tie end-to-end to completely enclose the area. Line segments are a set of sequentially numbered coordinate pairs. No duplicate features exist nor duplicate points in a data string. Intersecting lines are separated into individual line segments at the point of intersection. All nodes are represented by a single coordinate pair that indicates the beginning or end of a line segment.

Completeness_Report:
All geologic units and line data were captured from Peterson and others, 1990; point data, such as strike and dip, were not captured.

Positional_Accuracy:
Horizontal_Positional_Accuracy:
Horizontal_Positional_Accuracy_Report:
Arcs are probably no more accurate than approximately 200 m based upon the RMS error encountered when transforming the dataset based on mathmetically defined tics.

Lineage:
Source_Information:
Source_Citation:
Citation_Information:
Originator: Peterson, J.A.
Originator: Berquist, J.R.
Originator: Reynolds, S.J.
Originator: Page-Nedell, S.S.
Publication_Date: 1990
Title: Geologic map of the Tucson and Nogales quadrangles, in Peterson, J.A., ed., Preliminary mineral resource assessment of the Tucson and Nogales 1° x 2° quadrangles, Arizona (plate 1) U.S. Geological Survey Open-File Report 90-276, 134 p., 24 plates.
Geospatial_Data_Presentation_Form: map

Series_Information:
Series_Name: Open-File Report
Issue_Identification: OF 90-276
Publication_Information:
Publication_Place: Menlo Park, CA
Publisher: U.S. Geological Survey
Source_Scale_Denominator: 250,000
Type_of_Source_Media: mylar
Source_Time_Period_of_Content:
Time_Period_Information:
Single_Date/Time:
Calendar_Date: 1990
Source_Currentness_Reference: publication date
Source_Citation_Abbreviation: Peterson and others, 1990
Source_Contribution: This is the major source for the dataset.

Process_Step:
Process_Description:
Southwest Field Office GIS staff/contractors procured a mylar copy of the "Geologic Map of the Tucson and Nogales Quadrangles" and a gray-scale scan was made of the of the mylar map at 300 dpi resolution.

A set of tics were mathmetically generated for pre-selected latitude-longitude coordinates then projected to the Universal Tranverse Mercator projection (zone 12) and the scanned map was registered to the set of tics.

The map was divided into ten sections and the line work was digitized and attributed for each of the sections in a "heads-up", on-screen fashion. A standard zoom scale was employed when digitizing the arcs.

Check plots were produced to check both line (arc) locational and attributional fidelity relative to the source mylar map. Line work accuracy was verified. The editor made changes where appropriate and the edits were entered. The checking/editing process was repeated until no additional corrections could be identified.

The 10 digitized sections were joined, edited for dangles and undershoots, and cleaned to produce polygon topology.

Polygons were attributed with the geologic (rock) unit label. Queried units, unlabeled units, and multiple labeled units from the original map were flagged in the coverage.

Check plots were made of the polygon rock unit attributes. The editor employed other published and unpublished geologic maps to resolve the flagged units. Geologic inconsistencies (such as adjacent polygons with the same geologic label) were identified and resolved. This step was repeated as needed.

The accompanying tables were defined and populated. Files accompanying the database where produced.

Process_Date: 19991201 to 20000830

Process_Step:
Process_Description:
First draft of metadata created by G.S. Pitts using
FGDCMETA.AML ver. 1.2 05/14/98
Process_Date: 20000927

Spatial_Data_Organization_Information:
Direct_Spatial_Reference_Method: Vector
Point_and_Vector_Object_Information:
SDTS_Terms_Description:
SDTS_Point_and_Vector_Object_Type: Point
Point_and_Vector_Object_Count: 2279
SDTS_Terms_Description:
SDTS_Point_and_Vector_Object_Type: String
Point_and_Vector_Object_Count: 6621
SDTS_Terms_Description:
SDTS_Point_and_Vector_Object_Type: GT-polygon composed of chains
Point_and_Vector_Object_Count: 2280

Spatial_Reference_Information:
Horizontal_Coordinate_System_Definition:
Planar:
Grid_Coordinate_System:
Grid_Coordinate_System_Name: Universal Transverse Mercator
Universal_Transverse_Mercator:
UTM_Zone_Number: 12
Transverse_Mercator:
Scale_Factor_at_Central_Meridian: 0.9996
Longitude_of_Central_Meridian: -111.0
Latitude_of_Projection_Origin: 0.0
False_Easting: 0.0
False_Northing: 0.0
Planar_Coordinate_Information:
Planar_Coordinate_Encoding_Method: coordinate pair
Coordinate_Representation:
Abscissa_Resolution: 20.
Ordinate_Resolution: 20.
Planar_Distance_Units: Meters
Geodetic_Model:
Horizontal_Datum_Name: North American Datum of 1927
Ellipsoid_Name: Clarke 1866
Semi-major_Axis: 6378206.4
Denominator_of_Flattening_Ratio: 294.98

Entity_and_Attribute_Information:
Overview_Description:
Entity_and_Attribute_Overview:

The digital database for the geologic map of the Tucson and Nogales quadrangles consists of one ArcInfo arc and polygon coverage, which produces an arc attribute table (tn250k.aat), and a polygon attribute table (tn250k.pat). There are also five accompanying INFO data files, tn250k.con, tn250k.lgu,

tn250k.ref, tn250k.ru, and tn250k.str, as look-up tables
containing additional attributions for arcs and polygons.

The ArcInfo coverage, tn250k, contains geologic contacts (linecodes less than 100) which relate to the tn250k.con table, geologic faults (linecodes 100 to 600) which relate to the tn250k.str table, linear geologic (rock) units (linecodes greater than 600) which relate to the tn250k.lgu table, areal (polygonal) rock units which relate to the tn250k.ru table. All features relate to the tn250k.ref table which contains information on the source.

Entity_and_Attribute_Detail_Citation: none

A detailed description of the attributes for the digital database of the geologic map of the Tucson and Nogales 1:250,000-scale quadrangles are given in the text of Open-File Report 01-275, available in Adobe PDF on the World Wide Web at http://geopubs.wr.usgs.gov/open-file/of01-275.

Distribution_Information:
Distributor:
Contact_Information:
Contact_Organization_Primary:
Contact_Organization: U.S. Geological Survey Information Services
Contact_Address:
Address_Type: mailing and physical address
Address: Box 25286
City: Denver
State_or_Province: CO
Postal_Code: 80225
Country: U.S.A.
Contact_Voice_Telephone: (303)202-4700
Contact_Facsimile_Telephone (303)202-4188
Contact_Instructions: (Contact via email)
Contact_Electronic_Mail_Address: (distributor email)

Distribution_Liability:

The U.S. Geological Survey (USGS) provides these geographic data "as is." The USGS makes no guarantee or warranty concerning the accuracy of information contained in the geographic data. The USGS further makes no warranties, either expressed or implied, as to any other matter whatsoever, including, without limitation, the condition of the product, or its fitness for any particular purpose. The burden for determining fitness for use lies entirely with the user. Although these data have been processed successfully on computers at the USGS, no warranty, expressed or implied, is made by the USGS regarding the use of these data on any other system, nor does the fact of distribution constitute or imply any such warranty.

In no event shall the USGS have any liability whatsoever for payment of any consequential, incidental, indirect, special, or tort damages of any kind, including, but not limited to, any loss of profits arising out of use of or reliance on the geographic data or arising out of the delivery, installation, operation, or support by USGS.

This digital geologic map database of the Tucson and Nogales 1:250,000-scale quadrangles, AZ, is not meant to be used or displayed at any scale larger than 1:250,000 (for example, 1:100,000 or 1:24,000).

Metadata_Reference_Information:
 Metadata_Date: 20000927
 Metadata_Review_Date: 20001001
 Metadata_Future_Review_Date: 20001002
 Metadata_Contact:
  Contact_Information:
   Contact_Organization_Primary:
    Contact_Organization: U.S. Geological Survey
    Contact_Person: G. Stephen Pitts
   Contact_Position: GIS Lab coordinator
   Contact_Address:
    Address_Type: (mailing and physical address)
    Address: 520 N. Park Ave, Suite 355
    City: Tucson
    State_or_Province: Arizona
    Postal_Code: 85719
    Country: USA
   Contact_Voice_Telephone: 520.670.5511
   Contact_Facsimile_Telephone: 520.670.5571
   Contact_Electronic_Mail_Address: bear@usgs.gov
 Metadata_Standard_Name: FGDC Content Standards for Digital Geospatial Metadata
 Metadata_Standard_Version: FGDC-STD-001-1998
 Metadata_Access_Constraints: none
 Metadata_Use_Constraints: none

Lightning Source UK Ltd.
Milton Keynes UK
UKOW04f0008250117
292798UK00013B/103/P